fields of wonder

fields
of
wonder

ROD McKUEN

CHEVAL BOOKS

RANDOM HOUSE

Published May 4, 1971
Third Printing, October 1971

This is a book for Nan

"... I only know how true it is; that
love is a chain of love, as nature
is a chain of life."

TRUMAN CAPOTE
The Grass Harp

author's note

Done to death by deadlines, other people's clocks and needs, I took a year to think about this book before I started writing it.

Though it was begun in London, continued in Mexico and finally finished back in California, *Fields of Wonder* is not a collection, but a single thought. More and more I think that most of us have only one or two things to say. This is an amplification of what I might have said before and the beginning of what I'll say next time around.

I write with love; and a heart bright red is easier to hit than some crouched black target. Even if I could, I wouldn't have it any other way.

R.M.
February 1971

contents

Prologue

CLOSE WATCH

1.

I began by loving nobody.

Then nobody's face
became the face of many
as I traveled not to Tiburon or Tuscany
but battled back and forth
between the breasts and thighs
of those who fancied for a time
my forelock and my foreskin.

If they could overlook my acne
and the inch I lacked
to carry them to heaven,
I too could deal in charity
forgetting how their faces
always seemed to be the same
and thinking only how their thighs
were rowable and readable
and right for me and wrong for me.

See the stars.
Count them.
Watch the stars go sailing
through thc sky.

And as the stars
move through the heavens
preordained and predestined,
so too the faces in the street
file by as if by prearrangement.

2.

Now they're everywhere,
in cars with tops down,
stopped at red lights
or whizzing by at glider speed
toward some intersection
            in their lives
that I'll not share.

            My God,
when seeing them
my car can barely hug the road.

Barefoot and barelimbed on beaches
they hump white waves
and disappear as lovers
in the final feathered plunge.

Can this be a ballgame now
or some new choreography
that makes them leap and limbo
through the sand?

Are they innocent
of what they do to me
or am I meant to be
audience and umpire too?

I'd gladly be their volleyball
and call it victory
each time I bounced against
their beach brown bodies.

Whatever battering a beach ball takes
I'd receive with grace,
and some thanksgiving.

If they covered up
on summer evenings
I'd roam the waterfront at will,
but while they bulge and burst and boast
I stay home for safety's sake
(my own and theirs).

Bartok's blessed the Gramophone
with music of another kind
though even he cannot wall out
             my mind's percussion.

FIELDS OF WONDER

One | PASTURES

PASTURES GREEN | PAVEMENTS GREY

I discover.
      I project.
Or anyway I do attempt
to keep an open eye
even when brick sidewalks
are the pastures that I cross.

A beach in Sanford.
A road past clapboard buildings
or wildflowers groping
through the greyness of Gstaad,
might hide or even be
a field too wonderful to pass
            or miss.

Only when we pause to wonder
do we go beyond the limits
of our little lives.

Steep stairs in Amsterdam
or alleyways in Athens
can be meadows of amazement
as surely as familiar leas at home
can qualify as fields of wonder.

I know that
and so I pack with care,
whether it's my pocket
or my suitcase.

Fields take cultivation,
but it must come slow,
unhurried by the tractor's tread.
Good farmers don't harass the ground
until the ground is ready.
And just as only experts
have the means to teach us hate,
farming is an art form too.

So whether planting love
or lima beans
the careful man goes carefully
down his furrows.

MARDI GRAS

A mardi gras
is running riot in my head
made of goats on Spanish hills
whitewashed houses seen from trains
and bulls that run down pastures
still not green.

A mardi gras made of noise
and Christian names
not given and not learned
at the unmasking.

Whether I'm confetti killed
or thumped to death by noise
I ask that you believe
I wear no favor hat
        or mask
when I come chasing after you.

Love I wear
As open as a wound,
a mad mistake I know
but love, like Lent,
only comes to those of us
who still believe.

In loving
the only banner we can hoist
is love itself.

Excelsior!
I take this hill—
but with a white flag only.

You may tear my life
        but not my flag.

SUNSET

I wish nothing now
except to stay here spent
even as the day.

These arms the road's end
and your tired, tired face
already reaching into sleep
the climax of the climax.

Somewhere there are lovers
by blue rivers
going up steps hopeful
to a hundred foreign rooms.
I wish them well
for I have walked along my river
and found my room,
without the aid of any banister
I could in truth describe.

CIRCLES AND RHYMES

Your name
and your anatomy
have rhymed
        and somersaulted
in my mind all Spring

My eyes
were always open wide
beneath your eiderdown
except when you moved forward
to survey the circles
        you helped make there.

GAMES

When we tagged through trees
or raced the ridges
you'd never let me be
        the first one there.

I have no complaints.
I play to win
even when I know
the battle's hopeless.

WHAT IS IT?

Cloud formations
on a given day
and wondering
if you've seen them too
are enough to make a morning
pass for me.

Was your day
filled with wanting,
or the needlepoint of knowing
that I waited
and that I wait for you?
I did.
I do.

Swing safely home to me,
          come evening.
Make room for me
within your life
and I'll make room for you
within my arms.

If you don't know algebra
or *Alice by the Fire,*
or even why some roses
fail to climb the wall,
ask the question of me.
Never be afraid to say,
What is it?

Two | SUMMER

I AM BEING LED THROUGH LIFE

I love with such a passion now
that death is imminent,
for what I love is easily
so true to me
that God would hardly
let me know the pleasure of it,
even one more day.
No man could have such happiness
and still be left to walk this good green earth.

I so dedicate what life I have
to you I love
        and pray you spend it generously
on what you love and what you'll come to love.

Fields of wonder
are the places God goes walking,
I found them by mistake and I've trespassed.

A mystic I am not
and yet I meditate again
amid the London morning
hoping that my thoughts
go back to California.
I cannot cable love
nor would I.
You must assume
        you must believe
that seven thousand miles
and more than seven hours' reach away
I am reaching out just now.

To the far fields I have gone,
down along the sea
above the hills and back again
thinking I was running
new ground all the time—
learning only now
that all those wondrous fields
are meadows that a new lifetime
would not last long enough
to take me through.

Never mind.

I've will enough to make
as many journeys as I can
in the name of love and longing,
and years to pay for time I've wasted.

I am not sure
what waits beyond the block
but I'll travel down the street
            to have a look
        if need be.

Amen to what I knew before,
I thought that I was living.
No doors have opened up for me
and no new windows on the world
        only life itself.

I am being led through life
willingly and wide awake.
Your tongue has given birth to me
as surely as my mother thought she did.

ROME ITSELF

I carry
down between my legs
        Rome itself,
for you love Rome
and I would drive Rome into you
or drive you into Rome.

This room your coliseum
till you board your plane.
These arms your forum,
        cat's included.

Self propelled am I
between the morning
and the midnight
I glide along your groin
and earn my wings
by testing out your thighs
like some new willful Wiley Post.

My flight is not away
not to or from.
Above you, below you—
I soar around you
and perch upon your second pillow.

I have no need
for such mechanical devices
as winged shoes or wings.
I am made uncommon by the need to know you
and thereby come to know myself.

Rome
though in the distance
is no farther than the dresser
and not so far away
that I can't take you there.

For me the Spanish Steps
are centered on your tongue
and Caesar could content himself
with California wine
had he your eyes to follow
and your breath to capture
with his own breath.

We'll go to Rome
as slowly as you like
and be there by tonight.

WILL

I want love
for those I love
to come from all sides
not just selfish me.

If the moon can rise for me
it ought to rise for those
who comfort me, direct or indirectly,
banked by paths that take the dreamer home
even when the dreamer doesn't know
that I have willed his pleasant journey.

INITIAL VOYAGE

No one's moved the road for me
and no one's found a way
to beat the brush down
      through the woods
or make the brambles
snap back safely and on cue.

No clearing in the woods
awaits my coming,
      foot or horseback,
except the clearing that I make myself.

But the path to you
was never easy
and the road that led me this far
        had no lamps
    to light it.

So credit me with being
Chris Columbus for ten years
and never giving up till now.

Where once I hailed the masts
that bobbed above horizons
as my sailor kin
I picture them as rafts
in readiness just now,
not even knowing why.

Later ask the first mate of the Nina,
or the Pinta's engineer
they'll tell you how I smiled
even as I walked the plank.

And when I rolled upon the waves,
seaweed still between my ears,
ask them if I frowned
even when the friendly sharks
were chewing on what brains I had
before I started loving you.
They'll tell you no.
They'll tell you that I let the sea
Envelop me as I enveloped you.

LAND'S END

Passers-by do still pass by
and short of keeping you
face down forever
I have to run the risk
when we go walking
of seeing wars flare up
on battlefields as yet unmarked.
If I must parade you
as the entry in my midnight life
or show you to the sunlight
unmarked by my tattoo of ownership,
I'll do so proudly
and without a chain.

I have in common with all men
a lump in swimming trunks
and most of us have freckles
on our shoulders.

Men are men.
The worst of us are lovely
        in the dark.
All of us are vulgar
when you've pulled aside
the final veil.

Some of us are gentle
after four o'clock.
Some of us are poor
in pride or pocket.
Some of us can make you rich
in plain or fancy rooms—
currency not being comfort
only given circumstance.

All of us,
and that's to each man,
need you more than you need us,
we know that
and you know it too.

Three | TRAVELING THROUGH WINTER

PLANTER'S MOON

The moment
that the planter's moon
started down across your back
and promised me a harvest
great and good,
I knew that I had crossed
a different kind of field.
Greener than the ones
I'd trampled through before.

And if not safe
from all those hidden holes
and eyes lately
gathered in a crowd,
curious and hoping for the accident,
I knew it would be different.

I've kept my distance,
trying hard to keep the rules
and never violate the boundaries.
There were fences that I leapt
and some that I slid under,
even when I knew I'd tear my pants.
Not equipped with hook and ladder
I scaled walls and crept through windows
and burst through barricades
          and balustrades
as sure as any second-story man,
as certain as a centipede
all systems working.

I'd keep my arms spread wide.

I teetered on a tightrope,
          stretched between
your *sometimes* need for me
and tied securely
          by my *always* need for you.
Balancing,
          always balancing.
One foot before the other
down the rails and roads.

PASTORAL

Finally the wind has finished
piling up November leaves.
        Now it turns
to drive the snow in drifts
        along
                the
                        fences
of December farms.

The cattle come slow
        or not at all.
They scratch their backs
against the barnyard doors.
Their dialogue,
even as they chew their endless cud,
is low and mournful.

The lazy longhorns,
down the pasture
venture outside only
for a cooling taste of snow.
The wise among them
stay inside the shed
switching tails at what few flies
now survive the early winter.

Lie back.
The wind is on the move.
Till the bare tree limbs
stand still again
we've no need to move at all.

Turn not away from me.
But if you turn toward me,
do it in a lazy way
                    and slow.

Let me sleep a minute more.
When the coffee starts to perking,
come to me with smiles.

VERMONT

However small this time
let me catch it
        in my teeth
holding it as it holds me
tightly and for now.

If the snow
runs faster than we planned
I'll hold on when you let go
and lead you back again
through that powdered Vermont snow.

A WIND

You could feel the rain
before it came,
        the signals were that good.

At first the wind
then follow the leader
leaves and twigs
until the rain in earnest
smashed them to the ground.

And then your footsteps
slow and steady,
going down the walk, away.

AFTERWARD

The dandelion hasn't yet
been known to make a choice
between the pasture and the lawn
and love's as blind
        to rank or right
as politicians are to pulse beats.

Only desperation
cuts through everything.

Know that I'm a desperate man
        when in your arms—
and more so when away.
I wind my watch
when it needs no winding.
I puzzle harder puzzles
than my mind can comprehend.
By these simple acts
I manage for a time
to ward off facing
yet another confrontation
        with your absence.

How is it that I've come to this
unable once again to fill up
even one more day alone?

TEN BY TEN

In ten years
of watching you
and never knowing
that I'd share
     your Christmas bed,
I'd learned to live
with just the want.

Now with no point of reference
but your arms,
I can't go back.

BRAHMS

The clock was running down
and I had taken no precaution
for the coming night.
All the while
your arms were disengaging,
your smile receding
and your touch not tender and not there.

Then—
  (Please don't ask me
    what the hour was)
It must have been
within the Brahms
you went to sleep unsmiling.

If I knew
then I'd forgotten
that we were loving
        at your option
entangling at your convenience
and elevating one the other
only just by your design.

Unprepared I was
        and am
when any door
I thought I helped to open
closes while I look
        the other way.

CLOSER WATCH

1.

No speeches have been written for us
and so we never speak.
But still they move in front of me.
Unmet. Detached.
What common language
could we know
I wonder.
What words of sensibility are left.

Old hellos and salutations
now snap back through jaws
as easily as they once jumped out.

Conversation
if it lives somewhere,
must be bitten off in Braille
or spoken in a code
but never passed
from hand to hand.

Do I sound as though
I've been out seeking love again?
I have.
                    But more.
I've seen it everywhere
and I go on seeing it.
In unmarked cars
as well as underneath
a well-worn badge.
In faces not lit up by firelight
but glowing from the inside out.

I ache so much from love
I've seen but not yet shared
that I groan inside
        not from periodic hunger
but from habit.

Breathing
other than my own
can now make any room
as painful as unanswered prayers must be
for those to whom religion is the cord of life.

Once or twice
a face comes near,
and I look up
        and then look down.

2.

I am speaking here
to you and to
an unmet, unseen friend
who one day will fathom for me
yet another why.

Special mysteries
do not worry me as much
as what we do
to one another
beneath love's seeming soft veneer
while acting out the actions
we'd have acted out on us.

Watching you rise up
on elbows at the beach
as the long, lean men
pass by in faded jeans,
I am suddenly aware of age.
Not mine, but yours.

You look to be
not fifty, but not fifteen any more
and though I'm not at odds
with wrinkles or with years
a love that grows old over night
can hardly be a source of comfort.

I know that there are kinds
of crooked looks and crow's-feet
that modern make-up cannot hide.
And no reflected sun
however meaningful or kind
can screen away indifference
and the mind's projection
past the now beloved's eyes
to phantom figures down the street.

These things are all so true
that lovers know them always
without the benefit
        of any prophet's eye.

The sawdust made
by two lives rubbed together
is as useless in the cover up
of changing feelings
as the kind spread thinly
on the floors of butcher shops
to blot out blood
        and drying entrails
from the housewives' view.

At sunset faces suffer jaundice
even if the eyes
take on a keener glow.

Losing love again
causes me to wonder
If this habit is just that,
        a habit
not another stop
along this highway
where lately, only lately,
the end has been in sight.

Is it to be ever true
that all the lovers
meant to crowd one's lifetime
will on sunshine days
become excited by what might be
or what might have been
instead of what it was
the first time out
that made them notice us?

fields of wonder

SURVEYING THE DAMAGE

DRIVING THROUGH DAVIS

I woke up listening
where swallows
had been known to sing
and I heard nothing.

The morning followed the sun
not the sun the morning.
And as this day slipped
from out the last
into the next
nothing happened but the grey
moving in to overtake the whiteness.

I find any sleep
that claims to be a sleep of reason
unreasonable and fitful,
yet each night I fall down
in darkness
all the same
wondering what new land
knows the sound of singing swallows.

I wonder too
at teachers who demand
instead of teach.

One man—a professor now
(a sort of poet once
until his talent dried and died
from lack of any nourishment
or truth or understanding)—
makes a proper living
out of damning me
because the God that I believe in
lets me damn no man.

He wrote that I
was fostering unrest.
So I am.
And so I am.

Do not rest until you reach
a pair of friendly arms.
That's radical and wrong for him
but right for those of us who love.

And I say kill no man
nor murder his ideas
before they've had a chance
to surface from his mind.

Let men think and speak
even that poor *white-haired loser*
whose thoughts are lost
on children he would chain
and minds he'd not mind plundering
if even that skill he could master.

Let him help to foster masons
at his school
instead of militants with matches.
Man has learned by building
but even superman
cannot see past the fire.

The clergy
who drum into their congregations
litanies that have no bond
with common speech
worry me as well.

Until my life began to move
across the hill and down
I was unaware that God
was such a complicated man.
He was never Latin for me
nor Sanskrit till translation.

I want a man
that I can understand
to govern me,
for I need love
and understanding too.
And so I hope that God the friend
and not the father
will come banging on my door.

Were I your preacher
your teacher or your dad
I'd ask that you hate no man,
but yourself sometimes.
That can be of use
if only in putting on the brakes.

Stumble if you need to
but stumble on your own ground only.
Consider any man
that you can help
          your friend.
And double friend
that man so selfless
as to offer help to you.

I'll never be a proper teacher
for I've learning yet ahead of me
far beyond my years.
But place my small brain
in the feeble hands
of some *white-haired loser*
operating still without a learner's permit
in the love of all mankind?

Not a chance.

One day I'll make a pilgrimage
to his dusty desk
if only just to take him
this year's calendar.

Surely all men need to know
what year it is they're living in.

VARIATION ON A THEME

Poetry is not enough
and rhyme no substitute
for reason
yet to every man a time
and to every thing a season.
And you can bet your Bible, baby,
you'll one day get your turn
for if you're seeking more than maybe
it doesn't take a fool to learn
that poetry is not enough
and rhyme no substitute for reason
yet to every man a time
and to every thing a season.

LONGHORN, one

Yes I know the score
and where it's kept
and how to cross the room
without a flashlight
and how to cross myself
when trouble threatens
convinced that *x*'s work as well as *o*'s.

But longhorns
are a mystery to me
as no animal has ever been.
If the moon drops in the water
will I pick it up again?

OFTEN IN WINTER

Often in winter
that feared but unseen hand
old banker priests can still depend on
to help them herd their flocks
up the steps of stained-glass banks,
returns dependably
to work me over too.

Christ knows my span of concentration
and the time to teach me lessons
is the time when I'm boxed in by grey.
For when the sun shines
what man fears God
or his one begotten Son.

Loving is the new salvation,
with Gideon the king providing bibles
for each final prayer and evensong.
And bedroom soldiers
on ten million battlefields
fighting nightly sword to sword
would not dispute their uncrowned king.

I presume
that International Harvester
can take its proper credit
for bales of straw and wheat.

But man must not forget
who fostered love
          and fed it.
He did.

Whatever moral tract
        or bulging bible
gave him rules and regulations
man aspired to love
and learned its practice well.

Just as man is good
at finding further rainbows
when the near ones fade.

What litany you use
I leave to you,
but let it be the testament of touch
            however tentative.
A Mass to keep the cold out.
At the breakfast table
        or your dresser altar.
Let us now proclaim
the new religion *real*
after far too many trial runs.

FOUR SONGS

These are for Charlie and Jef, not poems by any means, but songs—meant to be sung. Though they came with music, your music is invited too.

THE RIDE FROM OAKLAND

Does the A train
go from Oakland
out across the bay
and are the buildings taller
now that my life's smaller.
And can my life be lived again
in the same way it was when
I felt I had to get away.

Not that I'd go back, I wouldn't.
Even if I could, I couldn't.
I've invested too much time forgetting
to remember what it was
I set out to forget.

And yet,
does the A train
ride from Oakland
out across the San Francisco Bay
and would I lock eyes quite as often
as I did back when
passengers on trains were prayers
and San Francisco was a soft amen.

I WISH I WERE SEVEN AGAIN

Mama canned currents
and mama canned peaches
and mama washed clothes by hand
and us kids had more
than the people next door
for we had a mama
who played the piano
and taught us to read
by the light of a lamp
a sailor man brought her
from some foreign land.

And I wish I were seven again,
I might even settle for ten
I wish I could go
to the Saturday show
and take the bus back home again.

SUMMER COME DOWN EASY

Summer come down easy
so that I can see
just who I'm talkin' to.
For I've been talkin' to the ceiling
I've been talkin' to the floor
and laughing at the shadow
sneaking underneath the door.

Summer come down easy
so that I can see
just who I'm talkin' to.
I've had a conversation goin'
with a second-story window
and it's gettin' so I don't know
if I'm making any inroads.

Summer come down easy
let me see your face
drive me into August
or some other public place
and come down easy.

If you come at all
summer come down easy
let me climb upon your back
and spur you through the fall.

IF THE WAR GOES ON FOREVER

If the war goes on forever
will we look out in the dawn
and see the eagle playing
with the dove upon the lawn;
and will we hear the trumpets
mingled with the harp
if the war goes on forever
and the shouting doesn't stop.

about the author

ROD McKUEN was born in California and grew up in California, Nevada, Washington and Oregon. He has traveled extensively as a concert artist, a composer and a writer. Before becoming an author and composer, Mr. McKuen worked as a laborer, radio disk jockey and newspaper columnist, and as a psychological-warfare scriptwriter during the Korean War. In less than four years his books of poetry have sold in excess of four million copies in hardcover, making him the best-selling poet not only of this age but probably of every other era as well. In addition, he is the composer of more than a thousand popular songs and his film scores include *The Prime of Miss Jean Brodie* (for which his song "Jean" received an Academy Award nomination), *Scandalous John, Joanna, A Boy Named Charlie Brown* and, with Henry Mancini, *Me, Natalie*.

His major classical works, *Symphony #1, Concerto for 4 Harpsichords and Orchestra,* and *Concerto for Guitar and Orchestra,* have been performed by leading orchestras.

Mr. McKuen's hobbies include skiing, sailing and driving, and he is currently finishing an extensive book about the sea. When not traveling, he lives at home in California in a rambling Spanish house with a menagerie of cats and three sheepdogs—Mr. Kelly, Old Boot and Arthur.